I'm Ready to Grow

By Regina Wilder

First Edition: June 2020

I'm Ready to Grow/Regina Wilder

ISBN: 978-1-943616-34-3

Publisher: MAWMedia Group, LLC
Los Angeles |. Reno. | Nashville

Contents

PREFACE

This story begins inside my head. The words, thoughts, feelings have never been openly shared. They are the dark areas replete with treasure boxes that are rarely opened. I pick and choose what I let out and what is left safe in those boxes. Maybe experiences, emotions, and heartaches are protected because I perceive that my reality is vastly different from that of others. Sadly, it is not. And that is the other reason they remained closed for so long. Others, closely related and not, do not want my truth shared. They do not want to admit that the reality I express from the boxes is true.

I unpacked those boxes and wrote these reflections in a safe space. I tuned out the naysayers and those who wanted to protect themselves at my expense. I moved distraction, insecurity, and fear to the background until each was invisible. I am not sure how I found that space, but I will describe it throughout my reflections with the hope that you, the reader, can recreate that space in your context. I cried. I experienced panic attacks. I gave myself permission to feel and recover. I was vulnerable to myself in my quiet, safe space.

Dedication

This book is for every young girl who felt hopeless, afraid, or even casted out by parents, friends, family, or maybe even the child welfare system. Family, society, and media attempt to tell you who you are. Your neighborhood is where you come from. Your experiences can be instructive, even brutally so. But your life is more than what they tell you, where you are from, and what you have experienced. I want you to realize that your life is what you create it to be.

To every female adolescent whose voice and creative energy was thought to be stolen, I am here to tell you that the time is now to reclaim what is misplaced or hidden and change your world for the better. Use your platform to build, elevate, and make room for the next individual courageous enough to challenge the generational curse. Do not allow your past to poison your future. Remember, when life gets hard, and your shoulders are too heavy to hold up, stand up tall, stick your chest out and hold your head high. You got this! Refuse to quit. Someone is counting on you to make it to the other side. When you arrive, do not forget to hold your hand out for the next.

It is time for the world to know that you are here to stay. Your voice matters, your dreams matter, your family matters, your community matters, and, most importantly, you matter. We need you. I need you to share your gifts and passions with others so they can see professionals, survivors, inspirers that look like you and me.

My Story in Brief

My maternal origin was mired in welfare, drug addiction, and poor education. I could only be that. If you are from a successful family, you have no choice but to be successful. You have people that can vouch for you. They expect you to achieve to that level. In poverty, the same calculus exists. The circumstance is limiting, and your potential is limited as well. When you come from a lower level, you lack people in your environment to support lofty dreams. You have no one to support the belief that you can rise. You become a product of your environment. That could manifest as a teenage mom, a multi-generation welfare recipient, section 8 housing tenant, or a dropout with no career path. Tragically, the power of environment is so keen that a person could find themselves characterized by all the above. You have the power to change what happens to you no matter where you come from or your origin.

My paternal side of the family was middle class, with marriages, solid careers, and a start on the American dream. The question on this side was whether authenticity existed. I often wondered who they were behind the accomplishments and window dressing.

As a child, it is difficult to make a change. On both sides, you are being counted out. Either you conform to it or you overcome it. The only way you overcome is that you have a mentor, teacher, friend, or someone else that pours something different into you. We slowly become what is poured into us, even in the context of a deprived environment. When you add positive, prosocial, and progressive ingredients and bake them, the product is greater than what went in. You change the product by changing the ingredients.

I speak from experience. I speak from my pain, my suffering, my insecurities, and my dark times. My primary message is that I lived through them, and I still face the questions and challenges that they charged me with. Pain comes from the internal question about why I was given this hand to play. It is a feeling that I had much of. It is a question of whether anyone truly cares. They don't have to live it. Why would they invest any energy in my recovery?

Suffering is a suffocating feeling. It is the inability to breathe. I gasp for air but cannot catch my breath. If I do catch the breath, I questions whether I can hold on to it. I question whether it makes a difference. Insecurities are messages that I am not enough in every area of experience. In my roles as a sibling, friend, romantic partner, and all areas of life, the question is whether I am enough. Dark times are a cave without light or sunshine. Everything is dark. The process of overcoming to find light and joy takes time.

Desired Outcomes for You

My desired outcome is freedom. Freedom, the process, and the vulnerability are my three words of healing. Freedom is the ability to let go. You cannot continue to carry every bag. You are not required to carry every hurt until you die. The ability comes with time and help. Make sure you get the help you need, including professional counseling, to accept what was past and chart a future.

I pray this book brings you comfort, healing, and truth, yes, your truth to self-discovery and finding out who you are supposed to be. Not someone negative speech but the person God has created you to be. When you do discover her and allow her to forgive, love, and be whole, don't go back to the 'Generic version' but the new and improved you; the you that doesn't need advertisements to prove what their best qualities are. You are a winner, and I am cheering for you!

The best is yet to come.

Accepting that this was my early process in life, I can get through the why and use this experience to help someone else. I accept my truth and my journey. It was a part of my life. I don't have to be ashamed of what happened. Yet, at some point, you must let go of that dark place. My journey is my ticket to something greater. It was my journey up to a certain point. My learning to develop into something better and beneficial to someone else is another leg of the path. Replace the dark place with what you want to be there instead. You can now create realities. Use that power to your healing advantage.

Vulnerability is critical to the process. It is difficult to balance the vulnerability with my professional role as a social worker. Many experiences in my current life can be triggers. The key is to remain mindful of the therapeutic purpose of my encounters. I give of myself as I know to be appropriate. I care for myself as I feel it honestly from my center. Your journey will be different, but your challenge will be the same. You may be triggered but rely on your training in those moments without losing your ability to feel and process from your center.

Defending No More

"You can't change how people treat you or what they say about you. All you can do is change how you react to it."
Mohandas Karamchand Gandhi INDIAN POLITICAL AND SPIRITUAL LEADER

We attempt to defend ourselves constantly before we get to a certain level of maturity. We are taught that sticks and stones hurt, but words don't. They do hurt. But you can't prove who you are to anyone who does not want to accept your truth. If you are always attempting to prove, you miss the chance to develop. I read a quote. "If you understood seasons, you would never envy anyone." What we see is only a season in that person's life. What you wear in the Summer, you can't wear in the Winter. You must learn to live with what is happening in that season and in that moment.

Life is not easy for a lot of people, but if you're reading this, you are stronger than what you might feel today or tomorrow. Become stronger because you too, one day, will be able to say I made it to the other side when you become that doctor, lawyer, entrepreneur, relator, clothing designer, college graduate. Whatever you dream of, you can become. And I'm spirit; I will be there cheering you on. The win must be a constant assurance for yourself. You must become your own cheerleader. Assure yourself that you can overcome, you can win. When I look back on my younger years, it sucked, but I overcame it. Not everyone overcomes. Some turn to drugs or other unsustainable choices to suppress the hurt. Some linger stuck in the developmental phase they were stifled in.

The reality is that not everyone will make it to the other side. Not everyone experiences the healing and maturity. That is a hard pill to swallow, but I know you would be happy you did. When you accept your truth and your power to create realities, you are better able to see where you are stuck and stagnant. You realize that it is up to you now. When you were a child, you did not have the power. But as an adult, you get to make the choices about activities that will contribute to or impair your success.

Section I: Changing My Reactions

Chapter 1: 3 Critical Things

Genesis 50:20-21 English Standard Version (ESV)

20 As for you, you meant evil against me, but God meant it for good, to bring it about that many people[a] should be kept alive, as they are today. 21 So do not fear; I will provide for you and your little ones." Thus, he comforted them and spoke kindly to them.

Every young girl who felt a sense of hopelessness, afraid or even casted out by parents, friends, family, or even the child welfare system deserves a new perspective. Though your journey may feel like a bad storm that never ends, you will overcome and see the sun again. You ask God to end this pain. You ask what you did that caused this much pain and suffering. I speak from experience; I speak from my pain, my suffering, my Insecurities, and the dark times that I lived through and still face. You are not at fault for what has happened in your past. AND you are the reason for what happens in your future. Both are important for your empowerment. The challenge from this point to the next is to gain the power to realize, apply, and live within that promised truth.

"You can't change how people treat you or what they say about you. All you can do is change how you react to it." Mohandas Karamchand Gandhi INDIAN POLITICAL AND SPIRITUAL LEADER

Life is not easy for a lot of people, but if you're reading this, you are stronger then what you might feel today or tomorrow. You are becoming stronger because you too, one day, will be able to say I made it to the other side when you become that Doctor, Lawyer, Entrepreneur, Relator, clothing designer, college graduate; whatever you dream of, you can become. And I am spirit; I will be there cheering you on with forgiveness, growth, and abundance as the goals. Each must coexist with one another.

Forgiveness

Forgiveness would have to be there for growth to happen. The forgiveness is for the offender and for yourself as well. Our minds play a trick on us. We think things happen because we are bad people. You think, "What did I do to deserve this?" You must forgive yourself. You did not do anything wrong. Life does not bring fairness based on behavior alone. Generational curses are real. Occurrences, perspectives, tendencies, and addictions may be passed down. You must choose to end the cycle of hopelessness and lack in your generation. It is easy to remain in the past. Those behaviors and outcomes are comfortable. They are well-worn paths that offer little resistance.

You must have the courage to refuse the past circumstance that keeps you in a broken approach to life. Resilience is a fight for your happiness—a fight to be whole, healed, and holistic.

This allows for growth. The weeds that grew and suffocated your heart can be mowed away slowly. Your flow is reestablished. Growth ensues and abundance will result.

Accept your past and accept the person you are becoming.

Daily, accept that good thing will happen for you. Reassure yourself each day. Encourage yourself that you have this. The quote in my mirror is as follows:

Nothing missing.
Nothing lacking.
Nothing broken.

What we are thinking and feeling take forever to catch up and connect. We must be intentional in putting these together and operating within that reality.

My greatest challenge with forgiveness was (and still is) getting the perpetrator to see the event from my point of view. When you want to be whole yourself, you must realize that this may never happen. We don't determine the actions or the vision of people. We may be tempted to put more attention on the past to the detriment of our futures. As the famous quote says, "Don't allow your past to poison your future."

You may never hear, "I'm sorry." Some people do not know what it is to truly communicate remorse and compassion. Action is the primary currency of apology. They tell whether there is true remorse or subterfuge. But your choice must be to move forward regardless.

Our need for that apology is a need for self-validation. The need is a result of what was taken away. Whether it was respect, loyalty, trust, or something else, we want it back.

We may never get it back. We may be left with a replacement. The replacement differs for everyone. Create boundaries and limit the person who offended, abused, or victimized you or cut them off completely if that is possible. Never go back to what caused that pain. Everyone does not deserve to be in the front row of your life. Some should be in the twelfth row or not in the audience at all. We often place people (or allow them to sit) in positions that they were never meant to be in.

Growth

Growth is accepting the truth about who you are. When you accept, you resolve that you are not able to lose in any area of your life. You have no limits. You believe that you deserve every good and perfect thing. You recognize that no one can compete with you for what is yours. It is a foregone conclusion that you will reach, achieve, and experience what is for you.

Think Bigger. Often, it is easier to minimize yourself or shrink in the context of the world. We take much of our lives to figure out who we are and our purpose in the world. We wonder where we fit. This wondering is intensified, and the solution is stifled when we have people in our lives that constantly tell us that we are not good enough. That voice sometimes becomes our internal voice. We miss a definition of self beyond our names.

Something lacks in stages of life where we shrink. We don't get the nutrients that we need for proper growth. Love, forgiveness, trust, positivity, opportunity, perspective, and more are limited. Often, a fear of the unknown cripples. It is a fear of falling, and more importantly, a fear of falling upward. We know about falling but having to live and maintain levels of growth and development can be more intimidating. The fear of losing what we have after we have had a taste of it can be stifling.

Move into Power. My first conversation with myself was about proving the naysayers wrong. I wanted to achieve beyond what was expected of me. This was first, but this is not the path to wholeness. The naysayers maintain a hold on you when you continually reference them for motivation.

Another option is spiritual growth. TD Jakes discussed a farmer's method. You can't plant new seed on old soil. You must replace the topsoil. You must bury the seed far enough so that the roots can be strong. His quote:

When we allow the lord to shift our mindset, we begin to see that everything that has ever happened to us happened for a reason. If we look back at the sprout that pushed itself through the ceiling of dirt above it, we discover reasons behind our adversity that were previously invisible and unimaginable but now are suddenly apparent and miraculous when we arrive at the fruit-bearing stage.

Accept Your Contribution as Enough. We do not have to bring anything else to the table but ourselves. No contract. No judgement. Your deficit and your brokenness are acceptable. You can experience reparation and restoration. It is a constant expectation that better is coming. Matthew 21:22 suggests that you can receive whatever you ask for in prayer. You must take your eyes from what has happened to fully take in what is happening currently.

Trust for Something Better. It may not happen overnight. You rest in the comfort that you have made your request and intention certain. That better is coming. When you go to sleep, you are comforted. It may be easy to dismiss with a request for a million dollars. You can wait. But the nutrients of love, patience, forgiveness, and more are available to us each day. We must only receive them.

Abundance

If we experience forgiveness and growth, abundance is inevitable. Regardless of the hurt you have experienced; you can overcome and heal. Those who hurt you do not control that reality. You do. Continue making healthy choices throughout your life. Choose kindness as your default interaction. When you are nice to someone who is a complete jerk to you, they change over time. Stay in control of who you are. Do not allow another to take your peace from you.

Abundance is not primarily about money and material things. Those things bring capacity and capability. Ability is nice to have. But those things are temporal and external when tied to material things. We see people with great riches and toys die by suicide. They lack an internal abundance that feeds them.

Having a genuine sense of fulfillment through purpose, a positive regard for others, and a clarified sense of self is more valuable than anything else. The everyday assurance from forgiveness and the faith that comes from growth sustains your abundance. It is a continual and intentional choice that will help you make your decision about how you engage with what happens in the day.

In the face of things going wrong, what is left is trust. Trust that God will work it out for you. Sit. That is your primary action. Wait on the lord as counseled in Psalm 27:14. When we try to make things right, we often make matters much worse. The things that you physically see can change. You can see that it is raining outside and know that it will not always rain. We can see the sun and know that it is a harbinger of nighttime. Just as there are seasons throughout the year, there are seasons in our lives. We must respect the seasons and the fact that they pass. Waiting is being patient. Accept peace and clarity that comes in each moment.

God is not a magic genie. If that were the case, we would not find growth and resilience through the pressures that we encounter. Even if answers are not apparent before we go to sleep, we must trust that God will work it out.

While you are sitting, notice the peace and clarity. You are in a better position to move with intention. Continue to do the things that you know you are called to do. Stay away from "fixing" things. I have been in situations where I have waited, and I find that I don't want the thing that I was waiting for after all. I have found that I received things that were ten times better than what I was waiting for. I did not obsess or overstep. I did not overlook or rush the process prematurely. When it arrived, I saw it for what it was through peace and clarity.

In those times, when I threw my adult temper tantrum, I have been in a position I was not happy with. Had I waited; I would have been better off. Sometimes it is good to wait until that thing comes to full term. It can be a business, a relationship, and opportunity or anything else. Allow it to gestate fully and become fully formed. Wait while it works out. That is a hard pill to swallow, but I know you would be happy you did.

As you grow, please remember, "You can't change how people treat you or what they say about you. All you can do is change how you react to it." Mohandas Karamchand Gandhi INDIAN POLITICAL AND SPIRITUAL LEADER

Chapter 2: Who Am I?

Before I formed thee in the belly, I knew thee; and before thou came forth out of the womb, I sanctified thee, and I ordained thee a prophet unto the. Jeremiah 1:5

Let's start with the basics. If we go by what my horoscope says, I am considered strong, unwavering, and strong-willed. You know—bull-headed. I'm a Taurus. Bulls have two sides. First is stubborn and strong-willed. On the other hand, they are loyal, family-oriented, and loving. My siblings say that I am combative. They often get the horns of this bull. Sometimes people only see one side. It is easy for me to maintain that image because it feels like that persona is what they want to see.

I am not on social media to flaunt and flex. I only post certain areas of my life. I may not be there for four months. Then, I will post a picture. I like my privacy. I don't like people in my business. That's me, but I will tell someone that I'm close with about some things knowing that they can't keep anything.

Better yet, let us go by what social media say I am. I'm too fat, too black, too ghetto, too loud, hair too nappy. "Her butt is too wide and mouth too active from always speaking her mind." To be honest, I may be all those things, but does that define Who I AM? I may be a little rough around the edges, ghetto, and boogie at the same time. My family says that I have some "ghetto tendencies." I am impeccably dressed at work and may be bonnet-sheik at Walmart. I may stand in church like an angel after having cursed out a parishioner for something they did in the parking lot. But right now, let me take a minute to explain my vitals. I am 5'5, brown eyes with thick thighs. LOL.

I am just honest. I like quality time with my family, even the ones with character traits and personalities that I do not care for as much. Call me crazy, but I don't want to front or pretend behind a bunch of words on paper. I am often moody in the morning, so catch me at nighttime.

I relish family time, eating, listening to R&B music, taking naps, enjoying animals, re-watching Disney movies, and traveling when fees are low. I think I am as funny as hell! Oh. I can't forget, I have ugly toes, I think. I have two toe corns, one on each of my big toes. But yeah, I do keep them done. In the Summer, I cover them with makeup foundation. I would not say I am self-conscious about it. I just include it in my grooming regimen. I accept all of me even if some parts need more making up to present to the world. Some people like my style and others simply don't care for me. My thoughts on that? *Oh well.*

Yet, I adopt the opinion of others too much. I constantly need the reassurance that I am good enough, pretty enough, and deserving. My mind often tells me that I don't deserve the positives I receive. As time goes on, I am still discovering myself. But we can all say that if we are honest and open. I don't believe the totality of a person can be described in one chapter of a book. You must know that, to understand a person, you need to spend time with them and invest in them. And, even then, you will know more of what they want you to know than what you may want to know.

Seriously

In my abuser's eyes, I was an out of shape little girl with big lips and buck teeth. I was ugly and stupid. I wasn't going to be much in life but a mother on welfare with six kids. No one would want me. I would be placed into a mental institution because I wasn't fit to be with normal people. I would only be able to get a job cleaning the property of others.

It is not like I didn't have positive people in my life. I had an aunt that constantly told me that I would have to get certain behaviors under control, or I would never have a profitable adult relationship. She encouraged the better angels within me in her own way. My rebuttal was that everyone sees something different in others. Everyone did not bring out the same attitude from me. My attitude was different if I trusted a person, had a connection, or I felt a vibe. Without that, no foundation for critiquing me existed. I was not showing you the whole me. Especially when the people speaking had contributed to the trauma that structured my responses, I was dismissive of their reflections.

It only takes one bad word to negatively impact a child's mind. To correct that one word, you need a multitude of good words to build the person up. They would say, "Sticks and stones will break your bones, but words will never hurt." That concept is horrible. Words do hurt. Certain people can stab you in your figurative heart with results in your literal health. They have the power to twist the knife repeatedly. It is a hurt that seethes and settles into constant discomfort.

My Words

If we go by what men say, I am an Angry Black Woman who can't be submissive to her man. This is true, especially from the perspective of an untrained and inexperienced man. I am hurtful when I talk. I sometimes shock myself with the things I say. I realize that I often hurt people with words in the same manner I was hurt.

In my adolescence, I dismissed decorum with the idea that you could deal with me or not. You are loss if you did not. Now, as an adult, I have resolved to work on decorum and consideration of the feelings of others. Also, I have committed to identifying what triggers and pushes me into self-protection and attack modes.

One such trigger is birthdays for some reason. I am not big on birthdays at all. I am not sure if it was about my childhood birthdays, but we never had birthday parties and sleepovers. My birthday never seems to go the way I plan. Birthdays don't have a meaning for me. For my 30th birthday, I had a choice to go to Spain or buy a house. The choice seemed unfair to me. "Why couldn't my parents be rich?" It never seems to work the way I want. If anything, I would buy myself a gift. My mood is already in the tinder box of erupting attacks near my birthday. The trigger could be small. Someone could say, "We are going to celebrate this person (someone else in the office conveniently forgetting my birthday."

Oh. We are going to pick and choose who we celebrate. I say this to myself with both the frustration of birthday celebrations and the annoyance of being overlooked.

I finally got a job I had been hounding an HR department about. They finally sent me a letter stating that they had enough copies of my resume. They had me on file and would contact me when they were ready to hire. I gave them a few weeks to get the deed done. I was hired. I met four people during training. We celebrated all their birthdays. But curiously, by the time my birthday came around, I was in a different office; around all new people. My birthday was again overlooked. Typical!

Trauma-informed

I don't like speaking in public. I don't like crowds. Crowds can make me feel insecure. I question whether I belong. It doesn't matter how inviting the environment or the people are. I am unsure whether I have risen to their level. I feel alone often. Even with a group of people, I feel alone.

I feel cold on an island. My one plot of land in the sand isolates me. I feel that people engage with me for reasons other than me. I never feel like I belong. I am shy when I am in a room full of people I don't know.

I have realized that the energy of the environment doesn't impact me. I exert a tremendous amount of power on myself that supports insecurity. I often put the burden on others to make me feel welcomed and faulted them when they could not. It is easier to play the victim this way. It is a way of getting attention through the back channels.

I have a cousin that is like a little sister. She hates when she is not invited somewhere. When she receives an invitation, she makes excuses about why she will not attend. Through anger at not being invited and excuses for not showing up, she never has to show up or take accountability for anything. Playing the victim is a safe option while making yourself indispensable if only in your own mind.

If you want friends, the Bible suggests that you make yourself friendly. But I don't like being vulnerable. I don't want to feel weak and exposed. The greatest of fears is that those words uttered during the expression of my vulnerabilities will be repeated by someone to hurt me. And this is the challenge of who I am. Complex in my desire to have friends and cure loneliness while simultaneously resisting any exposure to hurt and betrayal.

I know many can relate. Trauma creates this dichotomy at least and dissociation at worst. My continued exploration of self is revealing the positives, the origins, and the triggers. My goal is to rehearse the positives to train a new inner voice. I want to acknowledge the origins and reclaim my power to choose now as an adult. I want to prepare for my triggers and hold them as real but not determinants. I can. You can too.

Chapter 3: Dark Times

The reason the world does not know us is that it did not know him. 1 John 3:1

Yes, we all experienced dark times. But we all handle situations differently. I was cooking dinner and really not watching but watching *Sunday Best* with host, Kirk Franklin. One of the judges spoke and told the singer, "Smile. Don't let the enemy change your posture or who you are." That stuck with me. I felt, at that moment, God was speaking to me. I have allowed people, situations, and tactics of the enemy to change my mood, attitude, and who I am in my own eyes and in interactions with others. To sum up what I said, I allowed my actions and behavior to go lower when I was under attack. I basically told everyone around me that they controlled me and my behaviors.

Dark times suck. Yes. I know. But I learned in my process of healing that they come to tell us something or to pull something out of us—a lesson that must be addressed and learned from at the same time. You may cry and feel as though everything is falling apart and that God has forgotten about you. I tried to form my mouth many times to say that I don't believe in God or his word when Regina's life is falling apart. I would say, "God, I'm walking away," as if he was going to open His hands and give me something because I had an adult temper tantrum. I think it is because I've become lazy and don't want to put the work into my own life. I have become lazy and wanted to be the victim in my adult life because I wanted people to pity me and understand that I had a hard life. But it does not work that way. Nope. Those lessons remained for me to endure.

Never Wasted Energy

Energy is neither created nor destroyed, the Physics professors tell us. And nothing that you endured in your life will go to waste. God will use it for your benefit, whatever the challenge. It hurts, but I like to think of every occurrence as gifts or messages. Horrible situations and terrible things will happen, but YOUR STORY DOES NOT END THERE! This message is needed more than anything today! This generation needs to hear it. They need to see that their story will not just end here with the hurtful memory, betrayal, and trauma. There is another side of pain called joy, peace, love, and healing if you hold on just a little longer.

I had to learn who God was to me in my dark times, not what everyone else experienced and recounted. Their testimony on how good He had been was not mine. Regina's story is not unique. Others have endured similar or painful trauma. But my testimony is uniquely mine. God kept my mind from going crazy from everything I been through. He kept me from harm when I purposely walked into it. He loved me when I was unworthy and did not love myself. He allowed me to rise repeatedly after every promise I made and broke. Despite the hatred I held in my heart towards others, he kept blessing me repeatedly with a career, financial stability, all the things I think I deserved because I worked hard. I did not deserve them. I received them because of His grace.

But think about it this way we all know someone who has been through some stuff in their life and lost their mental footing. We know of family members, friends, or celebrities who died by suicide, experienced homelessness, or succumbed to addiction. All those realities could have been mine. But that is not how my story ends.

Pain cannot last forever. And if by grace, then it is no longer by works; if it were, grace would no longer be grace." (Romans 11:6) I had to learn that there is nothing you can do to make you unworthy of God's grace. In fact, by definition, grace is a gift to the unworthy. God's grace is greater than your deepest, darkest sin. Wider than the widest gap caused by betrayal. More brilliant than the darkest trauma. God can forgive, bridge, and heal.

Mom Erased

My mother was never spoken about in our home. I was forced to call my grandmother mother. She would say, "Call me mother because I do all the things your mother didn't."

How could she? I always thought in defiance. *She is dead.*

I don't remember anything about my mom. She passed when I was three. All I have are pictures. I have heard people say that I look like her. I have heard stories in passing, but nothing of real substance. I know that she was nice and yet a fighter. She was much more friendly than me from what I have overheard.

My mom was murdered at the age of 24. The stories were told in pieces by family as I grew up. I looked up the news article when I was older. The police could never prove with evidence, but my dad was apparently behind it. He convinced a woman he was dating to kill my mother while we were in the home. My brother was two years old. I was 3. The woman went to jail. My mother's killer was up for parole in 2019. My brother and I received a call related to the hearing. I talked with my brother and sister about it. They made the point that she should stay in jail. My point was that we must forgive at some point. My siblings lament the fact that we will never experience things that other families experience with a mom. For that fact, she should remain in prison.

I feared turning 24 years old. I thought I would get run over by a car or be randomly killed. My grandmother enhanced that fear. Her verbal punishment to me and my sister was brutal. "Keep acting up and you will die at 24 like your mom!"

I didn't have a relationship with my father either. He was always in jail for other reasons, other than my mother's death. When he finally came home and stayed home, I was in the eleventh grade. We don't talk. I don't feel that there is anything for us to talk about. He has stolen my social security and committed other betrayals.

I got a car when I was of age. He volunteered to help with the car. I guess that was the way he showed he cared though he never remembers my birthday date. He had a cart full of car parts. Apparently, he stole the full basket of items. He hurried home, driving the car into his mother's garage. The manager captured the license plate. They traced the car back to the house. I was spared only because the clerk could not identify me with certainty.

My mom named me Regina Wilder. Friday, July 18, 1997, at 12:30 pm in Philadelphia Family Court, I was adopted by my paternal grandmother, she changed my last name, and it became Boykin. I was renamed after her son—a man that I didn't know; a man who was never in my life; a man who was always in jail; and, a man who was not fit to be called a father or man in my eyes.

Even if I request a birth certificate, my biological mother's name would not be on it. It was like she was erased from my life, leaving no trace. I still have that feeling of Regina Wilder not being enough. I was forced to hold Regina Boykin. For all my achievements, I get to choose the name that is on the certificate. If I can choose, I use Wilder. This is my simple way of keeping that name alive. My maternal side of the family and the connection there is a solid support. I also do it in memory of my mother.

People ask what the big deal is about getting my last name changed. The big deal is that it was my mother's name—the only thing I was left with. Some people would never understand because we come from two different paths. But from a young girl in a world with no validation, it is a big deal. Losing a mother at a young age, you cringe at all the fairy tales and movies you watch, depicting the mother and daughter bond. From a child's first steps, to getting her first menstrual cycle, and first heartbreak, all the laughter and tears make for a full experience. I know that one special day each female looks forward to including wedding bells will have an empty seat.

Some authors suggest that the fairy tale is an improper creation made by children who have lost parents. My rebuttal is that we don't know. Every child should have that experience. As a social worker, I have seen parents who are drug-addicted and dysfunctional, but even the children who don't want to be home daily run back home if they are removed. There is something about the connection of home that draws every child back.

Feeling Lost

During my dark times, I find myself lost in the clouds. I shut everything out because I feel I need to be strong, or I can't allow someone to see me at my weakest. I've cried so many tears and asked so many times why I had to have this life, this path. And the answer I receive back every time is, "Because your testimony is going to reach so many young girls." You see? Our journey is not for ourselves, but it is valuable to others who are going through similar situation, wondering if they can endure. When we learn and grow through trials and trauma, we can give others the tools that we did not receive to cross on the other side of the river.

But we sometimes forget when we arrive at that destination. We forget what it took and how much we had to fight. We sometimes allow another generation to suffer with no guidance.

Why is that? I can be the first to say I have done that, not realizing I'm hurting the next generation that young lady will soon give birth to as well.

During my dark times, I find God's sense of humor funny at times. Each situation I have endured and overcome has been affirmed multiple times through people who I don't know, a song, or even a message. I know He realized that I need all that because I still have trouble accepting the lessons as useful to others. Yet, during my struggle and adult life with my spiritual walk, I've been taking baby steps to trust God, my heavenly father. That's hard for me because I don't trust my earthly father—a man I can physically see.

Trust is a hard thing for me. Being hurt and broken and not healed will leave you in dark times if help is not engaged. But my dark times cannot control me anymore. I have taken the time and opened my spirit to line up what the word of God says concerning my life like Romans 8:28. Trust is a process, but you will understand that all your broken pieces are working for your good.

Chapter 4: Home Life

And if by grace, then it is no longer by works; if it were, grace would no longer be grace. Romans 11:6

Home is where love resides memories are created; friends are always welcome, and laughter never ends. Peace, love, memory, protection, and safety are what I think of when I think of home. My home growing up was drowned in fear and clothed in hatred. We learned how to war with each other and always make sure you look out for yourself.

Crazy how a child can grow up and hate their own siblings. I continue to question how a parent or guardian could make her other children tease a sibling and call each other names like stupid or dummy. "You can't read or write." Imagine the trauma that affected that brain development.

Adopted

I remember when the adoption was taken place. At the time, we were already living with my grandmother, but before the hearing, she would ask us if we wanted to live with my maternal side aunt(s). I do not know if I did or did not because she always told us what to want or think. She would tell us we did not want to live there because they could not take care of all three of us and that we would not have a good life whatever that means.

But I remember the day of court and my aunts leaving the courtroom crying. We never really knew why, but we knew we were not going home with them.

Growing up, we did not see much of my maternal side. No relationship was ever solidified between us. I guess I did not know how to build one because I really did not know them. I really wanted and still want a healthy relationship with them, but where do I start?

My aunt from my maternal side made sure every birthday, Christmas, and graduation were a celebration. She was there to support all three of us. But, as it was told to us in our home, no day is more important than another. We live 365 days out of a year, not just certain days. As a child, you truly do not understand everything that is going on. But the experience is something you just never forget.

I find it funny because when my sister and brother ran away, they would always run to my maternal side. And still, to this day, they find a way to run home. A home maybe they call home or a place they wish they could reverse and experience again.

But I hope whatever journey they choose, it is healthy, joyous, and filled with much love. I pray that they pour into the lives of their children all the ingredients they never got growing up and that they be more to their children.

I pray that the cycle of generational trauma is broken. I pray for renewed vision, paths, dreams, and goals. I pray that a legacy comes forth and that each generation going forward from the Wilder family experiences greater success.

Portrait of a Child in Trouble

Picture a child scared to go home. Butterflies are in their stomach when they reach the top of their block. In an instant, they start peeing themselves. They knew they would not have a good day in that home. I do not have to imagine because I lived it. I was that child who never wanted to go home. I peed my pants almost every day. It was so frustrating to my caregiver that she made me wear the soiled pants to school the next day.

I once pleaded with my white teacher to allow me to move in with her and her family. On her desk sat a family portrait of her husband and sons. You know how they say picture perfect? That is what it was. She asked me why as we wrote notes back and forth. I told her I did not like my home and that she should adopt me. She conducted a meeting with the school for my grandmother and gave her the note.

My grandmother never said anything to me I never knew she had the note until it was time to go to bed and she told me to sleep on the cold floor since I wanted to live with a white woman. As I remember laying on the cold floor because our carpet had just been pulled up. I lied on the floor, shivering through the night without a blanket.

I was that child who was diagnosed at the age of 10 years of age with a learning disability: ADHD. I was told that I would never be able to live a normal life or live on my own. I was tormented with the threat that I would have to be placed inside a residential facility.

I went to school several times with a busted lip in middle school because my grandmother would punch me in the face for finishing a chore too slow, not doing something right the first time, or maybe she just was having a bad day. Whatever was the cause, it was non-stop. I remember a time when she hit me so hard the earring post got stuck inside the back on my ear. I had to go to hospital and have them remove it. The doctor asked me what happened. I said, "I pushed the earring in too hard by accident."

We never spoke with doctors alone. Even when they asked her to leave the room, she would still manage to stay in during any doctor appointment, therapist appointment, or any interaction with mandated reporters. If they did manage to get her out of the room, she would ask that we recount what they asked word for word. She would grill us for what we said and how they responded. She would threaten, "Tell them anything and they are only going to take you and your siblings and place you in foster care. Nobody in the family wants this headache." She would cut so deep that all I could do was cry and wish I could run away. I wished for Child Protective Services to take me away.

One of my aunt's from my paternal side once uttered to my face she wish that I was raped. Crazy, because this one was in church every Sunday, but wishing hateful things upon my life at the same time. How could one be so hateful?

Child Protect Services were called to our home several times. The worker would invariably comment, "You and your siblings should be happy that you have a grandmother who cares for you. Be happy that you live in a nice home."

Abandoned

We each have a perception of home because of how we have experienced homes growing up or in stark reaction to our home growing up. We do not often consider how to relate to a child who does not have a clear concept of home and what it may be. I would cry at night and ask God to kill me and bring back my mother so my siblings could have a normal life. I was convinced that my mother would have saved us from the trauma.

I did not know why my grandmother hated us so badly. What happened in the past that she could sleep good at night knowing she was destroying the lives of her own grandchildren? She seemed to love hitting or slapping us in the face, punching or choking us where her nails would tear our skin and leave nail marks.

I recall a day when my grandmother smacked my sister viciously. We were all in the basement. I think she was washing clothes and my sister was cleaning the bathroom in the basement. My grandmother went in for an inspection and the bathroom wasn't cleaned the way she wanted. She hit my sister so hard that she fell into the toilet and broke the lid.

I think she hated my sister the most. Maybe because she was the oldest. She treated her like shit (less than that), to the point where I think my sister completely checked out of her body, leaving her soul to wander into another world. In this world, she disconnected from life and its troubles. She never really had a healthy childhood. She was instructed to care for us. Cook for us, iron our clothes, and more were her duties. I remember times she had to stay up until the wee hours of the morning ironing the whole house of clothes only to shower the next morning and walk wearily to school.

My brother was the favorite. He got in trouble but not to the extent my sister did. I think she still fucked him over because he acts like a baby and needs a mother figure in his life. Even though he is very artistic and likes to read different books. I think he was dealt a shitty hand has well.

We all just deal with our trauma differently. I chose not to forget about my long-term memories or replace them with something I wanted the outcome to be. What a twisted way to create a sense of what love is supposed to be.

I think I always knew my life was not supposed to be what it was. I wished I was eighteen by the age of ten. I held a fear that could only continue to grow, and I hate that would never want to grow. My life was governed by doctors who sat and talked with me for 20 minutes, daily trauma, and a gnawing space where a mother's love should have been. My life was marked by negativity from people whom I called family, people who said the words, "I love you," but had not shown love in its true form.

Chapter 5: Siblings

Proverbs 26:2 Like a fluttering sparrow or a darting swallow, an undeserved curse does not come to rest.

My mother had three children. My older sister is four years older than me. I am the middle child. My little brother is one year, one month, and two days younger than me. It is crazy how all three people can live in a household together, but all turn out differently. I guess because God chose a different route for each of us. I do not know. The three of us surely have great qualities that we hide from the world. Or, maybe we do not know how to develop, display, or navigate them. Maybe we are uncertain about how they will be received or if they would make a difference. The way I see it: before everyone is born, life was already decided. The family who would raise you, the career you would have, if marriage or children were even a part of your life is predestined before birth.

I would not say my sibling and I are close. No relationship or friendship was truly really built growing up. I think we were roommates trying to survive the brutal punishment that we had to endure for 18 years of life. The ones we did trust always kept telling. Things we said always got back to our grandmother anyway. And that made my sister's life harder because she was the oldest. We knew too well the favorite line in the dysfunctional Black home, "What happens in the home, stays in the home."

We did not tell secrets to each other. We already knew the most important one. We all hated the hell hole we had to live in. But we shared in seemingly insignificant content and experiences amongst ourselves. We sat at the dinner table daily and ate dinner together. Little conversation ever took place.

We became closer as the years have gone by since our ordeal. We have created a tight bond. Like other siblings, we argue and do not always see eye to eye. Sometimes, we take a break and refuse to talk to one another. This comes with the territory. But we have learned to forgive each other and allow for each other's healing at individualized paces. Shared trauma is only our shared experience. Shared love is the foundation of our bond.

Memories

Yet memories flood my mind when I think of my siblings. I remember one weekend; my sister was cooking an apple pie. When she moved to take it out of the oven, she purposely dropped it on my left arm. When we tried to wipe off the scalding filling, my skin came off with it. We both were so traumatized that we feared waking my grandmother. We never told her.

I remember when my sister got her first job at Boston Market. She was instructed that she must work and give us allowance from her check. For us, it was a positive because we got money. For her, it was another day in hell. But she did learn to cook. And, I must add, I think she is a good cook. She worked but was never allowed to hang with friends, party, or do anything a teen would do. She never had a sleepover where friends would come over. I do not think we really wanted our friends to know how we were treated.

When she turned 18th years of age and left, a part of me resented her because she never came back to save me. She left. She was given a second chance at life with a new family who took her in. She lived with them in Hawaii though it did not last. I think it was hard for her to fully recover from what she endured. She witnessed my mother's murder, and her whole life, she was also told she would die like her mother. That must fuck with a child mentally.

My sister behaved like a child who was traumatized. My uncle had picked her up from school. She was the only one of us to see my mother's lifeless body. She is soft-spoken and reserved. She does not speak up or talk back. A conversation with her takes a long time as if she was processing every word. The trauma of our mother's death and what she endured with our grandmother took its toll on her.

I remember my sister had a cast on for a couple of her birthdays. Once, she was hit by a car while we lived in North Philly. My grandmother would antagonize her for no reason. I felt bad. She would call her out of her name so much that her growth was stifled. My sister trusts outsiders more than family.

My brother was probably placed in every residential facility in Philadelphia. Maybe that is an exaggeration, but not too far from the truth. At 14 years of age, I think he was seeking, discovering who he was. Meanwhile, he was crying out for a mother and a father figure. He is crazy smart and thinks he can debate anyone on any topic. He is especially keen on engaging me with his opinions. You do not have to venture a guess who wins those battles.

I remember when the first Krispy Crème Donuts opened in Philly. The donuts were hot and fresh out the oven and free when the red light came on. By this time, we lived in the Northeast section of town and school was closed due to a snowstorm. My grandmother woke my sister at roughly 6 am and made her walk through the storm to Cotton Ave from our house for one free donut. You heard me right, through a snowstorm.

I also remember the time we found a wallet on our block. It looked like the person just went to the bank or got paid because it seemed like a lot of money to us. I remember when we were allowed to go outside. My brother and four neighborhood kids would play.

We would go to ACME and steal fried chicken and hot sauce. We would eat it like we did not eat at home—stupid stuff. We used to throw rocks and stuff at windows until one day, my brother threw one too hard. It shattered the window of a Chinese restaurant, and they came to my grandma's house, demanding that she pay for the damages.

One glorious Friday night, when my grandmother was asleep, we ordered food from the pizza store that was directly behind our house. We enjoyed the feast as we watched television in the basement that was turned into a playroom, we never played in. We enjoyed pizza, wings, and cheesesteak. It was so delicious as if I could still taste it as I am writing. We never really ordered out, so this experience was a memorable treat.

Paternal versus Maternal Extended Family

We grew up together shared in many dark times and moments we made fun amongst ourselves. We have not been the most loving and caring to each other. I know we can blame the past. But no longer can I allow something that was meant to destroy us continue to chain us down.

It is okay to cry. It is okay to hate and feel as though you are behind the eight ball. You feel that no one will ever have your backs like you need them to. It reminds me of a saying my grandmother used to say to us. "No one will ever love y'all like me or care to." At the time, I could not see any fault in what she was saying. That was the reality I perceived. As an adult, I do not accept that lie. Each of my siblings and I deserve healthy, pure, faithful love.

My older sister was the child who was saddled with the chores of the family. I think my grandmother cared more for my brother than my sister. I think that was our generational curse. I know generational curses will be broken in your children's lives. Males were pacified and females were parentified.

I do not think anyone on my father's side really treated my sister right. She was always negatively talked about and mistreated. Granted children do stupid things, but sometimes you must look at adults who influence certain behaviors. Still, my sister is a complete sweetheart. She does not argue or raise her voice. I believe my grandmother stole that from her. My feeling is that she does not take up for herself. With our grandmother, our conversations were never about how our day was, how we did on a test, who our best friends were. I do not think those things mattered. The only thing that mattered in our home was making sure the house was clean. Our weekends included cleaning washing windows, pulling weeds, cleaning woodworks, and bleaching white walls. What a fun life!

So, I get why she left when she turned 18 and never looked back. Who would want to return to a black hole where your soul was drained systematically each day? Coping behaviors come from many issues, trauma left unexplored, and secrets that are never supposed to be addressed.

Deep down, she an amazing person with two beautiful children that love her dearly. It is something about a bond a child always craves from a parent. But I do not think she knows how to show affection to them or anyone for that matter. When being abused and used is all you know, it is hard to allow the walls, oceans, and mountains you built to be taken down so easily.

It was always a good time when we went to my maternal side of the family. The love was different. You felt the love, and it was shown. Granted people judge because they did not have the greatest jobs, or best education, or the cleanest home, but it was love. I think I would take the love other the dark night any day.

My message to my siblings is a message of growth. Forget the things that are behind us. Those things do not have room to flourish and impact our choices and moods anymore. Release anything toxic. I am my brother and sister keeper. I know I get on their nerves acting like a mother, but I see so much more besides the pain we each continue to hold.

I love you both now and forever.
I promise we will create a legacy that will live on.

Section II: Adulting

Chapter 6: Adult Hood

Hebrews 6:1 Let us leave the elementary doctrine of Christ and go on to maturity.

At the age of 10, I was already being called a bitch, whore, stupid, ugly, and fat. I was told I would die like my mother. Crazy, right? I used to tell my therapist I was scared to turn 24 because I literally believed the grim reaper was definitely coming for me. My mind would start playing out how I would be killed, shot, involved in a car accident, or pass away in my sleep. I used to think I would be raped at times too. At one point, I wanted all those things to happen because I did not want to live anymore. I had nothing to live for.

Adults and parents: Please understand that your statements are not always correct or warranted. They are, however, lasting especially if they are hurtful. Statements spoken in anger can become the soundtrack for a child's diminished self-esteem. These phrases can be the filters that cause all messages to be interpreted as disparagement.

Beware of certain phrases. The following are my top offenders:
"You need my help. I don't need yours."
"You can always leave."
"I didn't ask for you. They sent you."
"I'm only responsible until you're 18."

"You don't pay any bills here."

Trauma, right? Why should a child think those things about herself? Sometimes, or maybe a lot of times, I wished I could live on an island all by myself. I desperately did not want to deal with the everyday bullshit that occurred. I still have that feeling as an adult. I realize things hit differently when you are not a biological child. But crazy thing is that this same differential treatment occurs when a child is in child protective services care and custody. Some of those families treat the foster child differently from their own children. I appreciate and respect the ones who step all the way up and treat that child equally.

Moving Out

I purchased my first apartment in 2013 in Northeast Philadelphia. I think that was one of my happiest or should have been the best moments. It felt like a place. Not a home. Not mine. But cold. I don't know why. Maybe it was my energy or maybe I life felt like I was just going along with the flow. At that time, I was working with the school district of Philadelphia as a one-on-one classroom assistant. I was also attending school full-time.

I had a red, two-door Blazer with the tire on the back. She smelled like gym sneakers because I always kept my gym shoes inside. Trust me; everyone hated to get in because she smelled. She stayed in the shop, but she managed to get me to and from. I wouldn't drive her to another state because she wouldn't make it, but we had good times together.

I struggled to pay rent monthly. I never had enough money to buy groceries. I remember going to the gas station one day with $5.00 for my tank. The cashier was like, "Umm. Okay." The lady that stood behind me added $20.00. I remember not having enough money to wash my clothes. I remember all those things and more. I know what it is like for life to offer nothing as planned or to disappoint hopes and expectations.

You would think the first person a girl could call is her mom or father, but I didn't have either. My dad was around, but he was not a father. In my eyes, the only thing he truly was, underneath his designer clothing, gold chain, pinky ring, and earrings, was the man who had my mother murdered—a coward, master manipulator, and women beater living in his mother's basement collecting social security and storing food like a squirrel.

I tried to build a relationship, but it never seemed to go anywhere. It soon became a relationship where I would call and say, "Hey, can I borrow some money?" I never asked to have the money because nothing comes free from him. People say I look like him. I immediately respond that I don't. I never want to be associated with something or someone like him.

Ultimately, living on my own was too difficult to maintain. I moved in with a few family members, moving out of my place. The goal was to save money to relocate and clean up credit. I went from a queen size bed to a twin mattress on the floor. Trying to get back on your feet is not easy. I was reminded daily of my failure. It created a sense of powerlessness, following other people's house rules. I felt like a peasant among royalty. I could feel the loss of hope and despair, enduring everyone's favorite sayings:
"A woman your age should have more than you have."
"Why don't you have something of your own."
I thought, *I guess I don't fit the criteria of what a woman should be. If these people could decide, my worth would be in the toilet.* Thankfully, they don't get to decide. Sadly, it would take me more years than I am comfortable with from that point to fully realize this truth.

Living with unhealthy family members as roommates in your adult years is the most annoying experience. I think people get off, like a true, full-body orgasm or something because people love saying hurtful things. "You live in my house. Your rent doesn't cover my bills. Basically, I take care of you."

But wait, so you are telling me that even though I work every day, pay bills, car insurance, and save money, I am not an adult because I live in your house? These unhealthy, abusive, and soul-disparaging remarks weighed on me and influenced my approach to human interaction. If your family could be this cruel, you can't expect others to be heroes and emotional supports.

Creating False Unsustainable Realities

Relationships, both male and female, are hard for me. That guard is always up. I don't trust easily. I look for all the bad things first, so I don't feel disappointed later. I see the bad things, and my mind is creating the realities of an unsustainable relationship.

My mind tells me that I am not good enough. Good things can't happen to me. I don't deserve anything good. The only thing I am capable of is confusion, drama, or trauma. I find myself overcompensating for the insecurities I have. I try to achieve everything. I find myself achieving because I was told I couldn't. Afterward, I realize that I didn't enjoy any of it. I don't enjoy the process. I end up feeling that I don't have the emotions. I stopped feeling. I don't know what they are supposed to feel like. My happiness is numb.

I find myself thinking, saying that the next thing will make me happy. I am constantly chasing something. I don't know what it feels like or what it is supposed to be. If it was in front of me, I wouldn't recognize it. I try to get myself out of the crazy thinking and end up feeling isolated and alone.

Addressing my mindset is the only way forward. How you think projects everything in your life, just like a video projector with a lens.

If the lens is cloudy or obscured, the picture will always be distorted no matter what is projected.

In addition to mindset, I am gaining information to counteract deficits that I experienced growing up. Finance is a big one for me. But I want to be whole physically, mentally, and spiritually. You have a chemical imbalance if you don't have all of them balanced at the same time. I have been unable to furnish my apartment, pay rent, put gas in my car. I know I don't want to be back in that place. When I was in that place, I felt vulnerable in a traumatic way. It was the requirement to put my pride aside and ask for help. The people you are asking may not let you live it down. Some say, "Why do you have so much pride when you don't have anything?" That statement burns me up. Somehow people without anything should not have pride. Only those with something should have pride.

Who are we to judge and determine whether someone should have pride or not? Being broke doesn't disqualify you from some feelings. Some who are without means may tie the feeling of being less than with request for help. Because they made a mistake, did not have the option, or didn't have the information, people often lack grace and empathy when dealing with them. I hate for someone to tell me they did something because they love me or out of kindness. The time I don't conform to their ideals, they bring up the contribution they made.

At its core, this is an attempt to control you. To get away from this, educate yourself to create the potential for independence. Practice humility. Realize that certain levels or opportunities may not be for you at this time. Everything has a season. Build your career. Build physically, mentally, spiritually, and financially at your pace. Refuse purchases, relationships, mental taxation, and other experiences that do not support your ultimate goals of independence.

Transitioning to Helper

Beneath all that hurt and pain, somehow, I still managed to want to help people and still find ways to encourage. I think that is a good trait to have. Or maybe it gives me a sense of worth that I was needed, and someone needed me.

I knew at the age of 10 years, that I wanted to be a social worker and open up my own group home for young females like myself who have been undervalued, unworthy, and forgotten because I know how that pain feels and I wanted to help heal other, or maybe I still needed healing myself, and that was the only way I could heal from my scars.

I think that is why I close out and block my mind from everything. I ask God why he chose this life, this situation for my life. No credit was not a topic in my home, saving wasn't a topic, budgeting wasn't a topic, college wasn't even a topic. So, I learned things late, and I had to learn how to get my stuff together. But that easier said than done.

Thus, my vision and mission became focused on providing trauma-informed financial empowerment to woman and girls. I had not realized it back then, but I received an education in empathy, philanthropy, and humility. I learned how human kindness feels from the side of the recipient. I experienced how hardship and mistreatment changes a person so that they seek survival rather than healthy relationships. I forged a path of helping those with the life I was dealt.

Chapter 7: Loneliness

Isaiah 41:10 Do not fear, for I am with you; do not be dismayed, for I am your God. I will strengthen you and help you.

Have you ever been in a room full of people and felt like you didn't belong? This is a common thing. I know we have all experienced at some point in ourselves. This is how I felt a lot of the time, especially around the paternal side of my family. The feeling extends to my public interactions. I am not sure if this feeling is because of a preference, indicative of introversion, or because I feel an emptiness in my life. At times feel like I don't have a definition of life. Sometimes, I feel like I'm going through this cycle of various emotions: happy, depressed, moody, melancholy, and anxious. You get the point. It is positive that I recognize it. The feeling hits differently in adulthood though. Maybe it's because it's me, myself, and I in a big world. I have no parents, no children, no husband. I don't even have a damn dog. Lol.

Help is hard to come by with family because the time you do something or say something that's is not up to their approval standards, you will never hear the end of it. Mistakes are never forgiven. The past will always be present, and troubles thought past will always be current.

Family Business

Feeling like a failure because you haven't achieved certain things is insane and untenable. We expect certain achievements by certain ages from the world's point of view. But it hits differently when the observers are family. We share the same blood, last names, and holidays together, but through all those things our hearts may be obscured. Our sensitivities may be evident while our triggers are hidden. What if you could read their minds and really know why someone thinks something about you or interacts with you the way they do? Would we still be family or enemies with family ties?

For me, I have felt like I had nothing to give. Something so broken, in so many areas, cannot possibly give. That's what I thought. What did I have that would strengthen, encourage, or exhort? I thought my contribution would be as jacked up as my experience growing up. I gave the minimum as a result.

Everyone has their breaking point, where they are tired of being mistreated and abused. I play a role in this. I am ungrateful at times, entitled, and controlling. This often causes people to take steps backward from relationships with me. My inappropriateness is tantamount to giving my ass to kiss after someone has assisted. I didn't know how to truly be grateful and to communicate my thanks.

I resented the help I received because my upbringing was so hurtful. Anything that was given was given at a cost. It was offered as evidence of my lack. It was a reminder of my vulnerability and need which became shame. I am still learning honestly. I don't have the words to say, but my actions demonstrate the gratitude. My goal is to develop the words even as I work to counteract the historic trauma. I work to resist the need to make others feel my pain or be responsible for it. The solution is removing the shame of my need and finding supportive people who give without unreasonable cost.

What You Should Be

I think I've been told ad nauseum what I wasn't or what a woman my age should be. I was supposed to be married by now, one of two children. I wanted to own my own business and be retired from the traditional work world. These were goals that were made unrealistic or realistic based on my choices. I had struggles because I was not listening to wise counsel. I was not saving adequately. I was only interested in doing it my way. I felt that opinions were judgment. I came to that conclusion honestly. My life, like many, has a mixture of progressive and demeaning voices.

I'm behind because I'm 30 without children. In full disclosure, I can express that I could have had a child, but he/she didn't make it in this world. I made a choice when I discovered I was one month pregnant. I underwent an abortion procedure two days before my 26th birthday. As time goes on, I regret it more. I worry about whether I could ever have children in the future. I wonder if I changed my future, and I terminated the path I was given before that chapter could unfold. I question whether I am behind or whether I am without. Perhaps my childhood and lack of support have resulted in a delayed timetable.

All these things we as children go through impact our timeline. I fear that it also threatens to limit our potential. The development of positive internal voices requires an example of positive external voices. Great changes are possible when we truly have people in life, pouring positivity into us. When your brain is not receiving positivity, your growth is stunted. You miss phases of development that can't be backtracked.

For me, the challenge was not only about what I should be at a given time but who was with me—who really had my back. I think I accepted the feeling of rejection, loneliness, and abandonment because it was normal. I promoted rejection, closed posture, and limited interaction because that saved me from experiencing it again.

These are choices that no child should ever have to choose, let alone feel as the safe option.

My heart left my body at some point in my childhood. I don't think I ever knew how she felt because I never knew I had one. I never had the opportunity to utilize and nurture her. This was what I thought. I get lost in the fairy tale of what should be without realizing the heart that changes the calculations—the empathy that suggests that others should be consulted, the equifinality that demonstrates that there are other ways to get to the same destination. Yes, I had a rotten childhood, but I recognize that. I was sympathetic to the experience of my sister. I was responsive to my brother's challenges. I was fearful of my grandmother. I saw the experience as traumatic and unfair. I felt the hurt of being turned in by adults rather than being helped by them. And that, I can interpret as an adult, is evidence of my heart.

We say nothing lasts forever, but I can't tell because I still feel the loneliness. Maybe I still hold on because I'm over opening up, caring, or even loving something or someone. I have come to terms with the person I am and my right to determine who I will be without the expectations or requirements of others. Identifying and accepting that I have a heart allows me to follow it.

I follow my heart. I speak to God, and I do think He hears me because my story can't go untold. My mission is ministry to other women. That is my heart expressed in action. I must tell the next woman that she can be healed; that's her loneliness won't last forever.

Being Single

I feel lonely too, because I'm single. I am not saying that if I get a man, I won't be lonely anyone. I am now facing and understanding that I don't have to settle for every urge I get. I have matured to accept that chasing every urge will leave you even more lonely and broken than before. So, I cultivate patience instead. And that is the advice I give repeatedly. Be patient.

Often, I made it someone else's job to fulfill me. I felt happy because they were present. You must be happy for yourself. You must know what you like and what you don't like. Know who you are and continue in an ongoing self-discovery. Moments of solitude can help to put things into perspective. In that space, you must face your true self. You are not as able to cover up who you really are. I have often found myself doing things that I don't want to do because the person I hang out with wants to do it. I have lost myself at times. It makes me afraid of being alone. I question whether I will lose this person if I am my authentic self. I pretended to be something I truly am not for so long.

Whether you are alone or surrounded by people, you must be happy with or without. That special someone is a bonus. Interactions with people can make you feel good. A job that rewards us telling can be source of encouragement and satisfaction. And you must not relinquish the responsibility to explore, know, nurture, and heal the broken pieces of yourself. The most successful person may say that they are single because they are so busy. That isn't the proper phrase. Be single because you want to be single. Continue to make yourself a healthier version of You. Question whether and why you feel lonely.

If you are going to be with someone, you want to be with that special someone. A person that helps you to pass the time may be comfortable, but that experience pales in comparison to a person that enhances your opportunities, experiences, and reflections.

The opportunity is to view loneliness in the structure of solitude. This means taking the time away from people to explore You. Review your experiences. Reflect upon your likes, dislikes, preferences, and regrets. Find You without distractions. The 2020 Quarantine created a space for the type of personal growth that may extend from solitude. Also, take stock in wisdom regarding solitude and interaction:

- Accept you for you, whoever you are in a given moment.

Refuse to submit yourself for everyone's approval.

- Listen to wise counsel. Everyone is not out to hurt you.
- Learn to think for yourself. Cultivate discernment—the ability to determine the value and utility of people, information, and environments.
- Recognize that your cup of tea is the best to drink because there are people who specifically resonate with your frequency and vibrations.
- Learn the difference between being alone with yourself and being alone doing activities. You need both to develop a balance of introspection and fortitude.
- Don't be a slave to timeframes. Sometimes our viewpoints can be so mixed up and unclear that we set goals because we need to create appearances rather than develop holistically. Be gentler with yourself. Achieve in your time.

Chapter 8: Who I Am: Regina

Luke 1:35 …therefore the child to be born will be called holy.

Regina is a Latin feminine name meaning "queen." The signature symbol of the queen is her crown. The crown a queen wears represents rarity and beauty. It is a symbol of purity and innocence; of love and fidelity. It conjures strength of character, ethics, and faithfulness to oneself and others.

Parents are told that they should pick names their child could live up too. I wonder what my mother saw when she first laid eyes on me. She must have seen a queen who would one day wear a crown. She determined to set me on that path with a name befitting.

My Own and On My Own

My mother did not live to see me grow to adulthood. The feeling of loss leaves me at times not wanting children of my own. The idea of dying before they are grown frightens me. Not being able to ensure that their values and morals are intact is hindering. Most importantly, I want to live to make certain that they are well prepared to live without me physically, spiritually, and financially. If not, they may be left with people who could give two shits about them.

For a little brown girl who was called "big lips" or "rabbit teeth," not having a mother's voice that could whisper positive things in her ear resulted in low self-esteem and an early life of emptiness. I recognize as an adult that the lack in my childhood led to choices that exacerbated the disconnect. I don't trust easily. I have my guard up a lot. Some of that is based on my relationship with my father. But life, in general, has put me in that position. People don't give something for nothing. There is always a catch. In our community as a whole, we have been taught that nothing in life is free. We are private and secretive. We are isolated and often lonely.

An immense amount of wisdom and change is required. Many people have turned off their emotions and become colder. I am one of them. For me, it keeps me safe. It is easy to live in your bubble. You can decide what goes in and out. You are in control of your bubble. When you pop that bubble, you are out of control. I can say I don't want friends or romantic partners. I can control whether I am bothered. I can control my life. I would rather have control here than nothing at all.

This is the kingdom I built for myself growing up. This is the queenship I perpetuated into my adulthood. This is the realm I am endeavoring now to govern with more openness, grace, and gratitude. It is not easy, but I am changing the type of queen I am.

Penetrating Those Walls

It takes a strong person to penetrate the walls of my bubble. I don't like to live alone, but I like to be by myself. I don't want the environment of my family (husband and kids) to feel cold, but I don't like small talk. In my new experience of queenship, I reframed the analogy of penetrating walls to lowering the draw bridge in service to others. It is control still, but adulting that is monitoring the flow of people in my circle of influence.

You can choose to be whole. You can choose to be healthy. When I speak these words, I speak to myself. Not speaking to the 30-year-old Regina but to the one I left behind at ten years old. Even though we grow in age, we have left a young person behind in ourselves yearning for forgiveness, reassurance, and safety. When we find purpose and operate within it, we are the adult telling the young person within us that we can get through any obstacle together.

I have created a safe space for myself while giving the opportunity for help, collaboration, and engagement for others. I want to help. I use myself as an example because I am relatable. I lived the trauma, so I know what could be inserted to address the situation and offer a new direction. As I encourage others, I am encouraged. I want the women I influence; especially vulnerable girls to develop and feel confident that they don't have to seek from someone else.

Addressing You

I have been guilty of looking at the lives of others and thinking that I should adopt something about them. They appeared to be succeeding. Sometimes we get caught up in what we think success is. We think that our success depends upon adopting their traits, doing what they are doing, or interacting as they interact. This is not true. Success differs for everyone. Also, they may appear to enjoy a fairy tale life, but you often only see the cover of the magazine with no content inside. Their experience inside life may be incompatible with who you are. You must discover your true purpose and calling. It is certainly different from that of others.

The benefits of this achievement can be diverse and satisfying. Finding yourself is the greatest discovery. The skills of finding yourself apply to situations as well as life achievements. Of all my siblings, I am the heaviest in weight. Growing up, I was always labeled as the "biggest." I have worked to keep my weight down, exercising, eating right, and monitoring my weight. I thought about what it would take to entice a successful husband. *He would not want someone too big*, I thought.

My understanding shifted as I began to accept myself. I learned more about health and nutrition and realized the power of mind and metabolism. I began to focus on health and my doctor's advice instead of the pressures of other's judgement. I also learned to be gentle with myself. Even if I am no one's preference, I ensure that I am my own preference. I determined to accept myself unconditionally when I look in the mirror for exactly the person that I am. I am holistically healthier now. You can do it too. This is a question of identity. Answer the question of who you are by understanding who you will be as well.

Your revelation of identity begins with your situation. Identify the situation. If you didn't cause it, you can't control it. You are only responsible for your response and your healing. Engage both with gratitude, patience, and health as the goal.

Replace undesired behaviors with desirable behaviors. As you replace negative behaviors, you are creating a new environment of safety. If you want friends, you must learn what it means to be a friend—being true to yourself.

Be unapologetic. Be your true self. Realizing that all the "bad" things are not to be discarded. Determine which of them are yours, hard-won, and defining for you. Your choices don't have to change because someone doesn't agree with you. Take in wisdom and information. Filter based on the person you have decided to be. Don't live for other people contaminating your mind with what others think you should be. Decide for yourself. Then, filter.

Require others to address you in your wholeness spot. You are on a journey that will be rough at times. You will make mistakes. I no longer allow people to address me in the broken areas they knew from the past. I may be on a continual journey, but you must address me in that current place.

Adopt the mindset that you are the best thing out here walking. I make an effort to smile more, having realized that I have a great smile. I love my fun and sense of adventure. I'm fun to be around when I am not in my mood. When I am fully accepting myself, I am a joy to be around. My sore loser tendencies notwithstanding, my competitive nature will cause me to engage fully. No matter my situation or past, I remain compassionate. I can offer the best options, even if I have trouble accepting them for myself.

My Little Brown Girl | A Poem
by Theodore Richards

My little brown, beautiful girl
you do not see how cruel
the world can be
—I can see
this in your smile.
One day, they will try to tell you
that you are not good enough,
that your emotions cloud
the pure machine of Reason,
that you are not strong,
or good at math,
or fit to lead.
They will tell you
that what you are is not good enough,
your life, an exercise
in seeking their elusive approval.

You will probably know better than me
what to tell them.
But here is an idea:

Tell them that they may tear your heart out,
but they will only unleash the lion who lurks inside;
tell them that you may cry a torrent of tears,
but your tears are a raging tempest,
Bringing lightning and thunder;
tell them, little brown girl,
that their disapproval hurts you—
because it will—
but it defines them more than you;
tell them that you know
that the world spends so much time
hating you

because it fears your lioness roar
your thundercloud tears,
and that you are strong enough
to cry in this sad world
—to be brokenhearted—
without being broken.

Tell them, my little brown, beautiful girl,
that these long, sundrenched days
spent dancing to the rhythm
of the wisdom
that who you are
is already enough
is already enough.
But as the days grow short
and you come to know their fear,
you will tear open your heart for them,
because you will see
that this world needs
little girls who bring cries of thunder
and the courage of a lioness.

Section III: The Path Forward

Chapter 9: Rewriting the Narrative

2 Samuel 22: 25. God rewrote the story of my life when He found me pure in his sight.

We are taught never to tell household secrets, but I used to tell my classmates about all about my family. The fake one, not what I was really going through. I pretended that my mom was a nurse and my father was a police officer. I had two siblings and a dog named spot. It was a fairytale that helped me engage with the world of school. I guess I thought, if I believed a lot of that, maybe one day it would have come true, or maybe the storks delivered me to the wrong house. Don't act like you don't remember the cartoon where the storks are making baby drop-offs to parents full of joy and excitement.

The Opposite of Fairy Tale

I lived in a home where I was drowned in fear and clothed in hatred. That's the only thing that was displayed. My mother was murdered when I was two years old by a man that was supposed to be a father, a name I don't ever care to say. Understand my pain and hatred started at a very young age. I didn't choose to be filled with toxicity. Somehow, it chose me.

I only see pictures of what my mother looked like and heard people say that I look like her. I pretend not to care because it is a part of my life and heart that I cut off a long time ago. I sometimes prefer not to speak on the past, or maybe I chose to forget. Somethings are better left alone. We say we want the truth, but do we really want that truth? Maybe I'm not mature in that area, or maybe I think I will not like the truth that is revealed.

My mother was murdered at the age of 24. She was a life that wasn't even lived. She was just beginning. To hear stories that her children were in the same room that she was murdered and were discovered playing in her blood was sickening. What a sick mind a person must have had. To know the person who committed the crime is behind bars offers some solace. But an apology during a parole hearing in front of four people doesn't bring back a loved one. Confessing your sins before children who lost their mother in your act of violence doesn't bring back their mother. Your remorse, however sincere, does not replace the hurt and brokenness that was caused for three children.

But life goes on because living in a home where memories are all bad tends to offer little time for reflections on the past trauma. I have spent some time attempting to remember just one day of true happiness and contentment growing up. I am still looking at the writing of this book. One thing I can say is that we were in church every Sunday. We were active with every dance ministry and choir. I still can't sing or dance, but it was all for God.

My siblings and I heard the pastor saying, "Love doesn't hurt with words. Love encourages one another." I guess my grandmother was hearing a different message. Her home was none of those things that the pastor preached about. The result was a child thinking that a double life is what we all should have and indulge in.

I know your reading and your thinking wow what a messed-up house or maybe I must be all jacked up. The answer is not surprising. I was. I was hurt, full of fear, and starved for love. My deprived heart was turning black and growing cold. I perceived everyone through the lens of my pain, seeking my self-protection. As a child, I never trusted anyone. I never let my guard down. I always knew in the back of my mind that people were liars. People don't care about each other. Everyone is out to use you so stay woke. I was saying that before the song even came out. But believe me, my guard was on 100 and nothing could take it down.

Not surprisingly, relationships were not easy for me. I didn't know how to cherish or understand what a healthy relationship should have been with peers or others. You know that saying, "hurt people hurt people"? It is true. It's impossible to care and love someone when you don't even know how to love yourself or know what love is.

Revisited Abuse

Because I had to endure so much and was motivated to find my voice, I am the outspoken and active as an advocate. Maybe it was the experience with seeing my sister that causes me to advocate for others. I don't like feeling mistreated or less than. To many, it can come off as being combative, but it is the result of all I had to take in as a child and an adolescent.

I grew and moved out of my grandmother's home. I sought validation from men because I never had one to show me what my worth or standards should be. It's crazy that you know you want better and have so much to give even if you don't know what that means. Hurt people attack other hurt and damage people. I can assure you that I attracted many who could not care less about me but smelled my scares and unhealthy ways. When I look back, I'm not sure if love was involved in any of my relationships. Maybe I needed the safety net to escape my reality at the time. I found myself trying to make others responsible for my healing process and downfalls.

Finding a true connection does not solve the pain. As even good relationships ended, I was that same little girl looking in the mirror. I felt a lack of worth and despair that I would never experience anything good. I felt that nobody would ever want me. I say all this to say allow yourself to heal and know what you want in any relationship don't settle for what someone else says you deserve. Learn how to detect and walk away from similar experiences. Remember abuse comes in many different forms: physical, mental, spiritual, verbal, and sexual. You matter. Do not let anyone tell you different—not even that little voice in your head. This process has taught me never to return to the thing that hurt you.

Discerning Relationships

Young women, please understand how to play the hand you are dealt effectively. Life may not have afforded you a full deck. You may be short an ace or two. But until you truly realize that you are a queen, jokers will continue to invite themselves into your heart, masking themselves as kings.

Self-love is the first thing to address. When you go from one situation to the next, you smear your mess on everyone you come into contact with. You must evaluate what you want. You must determine what your definition of a healthy relationship is. When you don't know what you want and what you need, you become easy prey to lions.

In the wild, the lion sits on top of the hill lying in the shade. You think they are lying in the shade, but they are evaluating who the weak link in the prey that they are hunting. I believe men are naturals at preying on women that are vulnerable and unsure. To overcome this, you must make sure that you get the help to make you healthy and whole.

You can't reclaim a family of origin or the training that would have saved you growing up. What we can do is resist the inclination to hurry so that we are not alone. Don't be so desperate that you are settling for crumbs from the king's table. Hold yourself to a standard. Don't feel bad or that you are missing out on something. It is what it is. Don't let someone tell you that what you are standing for is dumb or stupid.

Chapter 10: Support

Nehemiah 8:10 The joy of the Lord is your strength.

A lot of my support growing up had always been from outsiders. Teachers, Mentors, Behavioral Workers who poured into my life and always told me that I was going to be something amazing. It is a special thing when you have individuals to pour into your life. Yet, one of the hardest allowances in life is to allow someone to help. I had my own reasons for refusing help or sabotaging help growing up. I have heard stories of pretended help that turned into mistreatment or abuse. In addition to the training that props up pride, betrayal can be a strong support for doing it all on your own. But accept two truths: 1) We can do more with help. 2) You can determine whether people are a healthy means of support or not.

I Need You to Survive

I used to sing a song in church called *I Need You to Survive* by Hezekiah Walker. The song is both a message about mutual support and a message promoting life. It is brilliant because that is exactly how real this question of support is experienced. Support provides a foundation for you to risk and succeed. Support also reminds you that you are seen and that you matter.

I need you; you need me.
We're all a part of God's body.
Stand with me, agree with me.
We're all a part of God's body.
It is his will, that every need be supplied.
You are important to me; I need you to survive.
You are important to me; I need you to survive.
I pray for you; you pray for me.
I love you; I need you to survive.
I won't harm you with words from my mouth.
I love you; I need you to survive.

These words had such an impact on me. People say that love hurts, but that is not true. True love does not hurt. When you use the same tongue that says I love you to disparage, degrade, and demean, you show how you feel about yourself. You are also not showing love. You are showing desperation—a desperate attempt to feel better about yourself.

True love is hard to come by. We live in a selfish world where people choose themselves without regard for others. That is what I'm used to. External support without an agenda or an ulterior motive was a rare experience for me among family members. A prophet rarely receives support in his hometown. But that lack of support is not the most damaging pain for many.

I know you all remember the saying, "Stick and stones may break my bones, but words will never hurt me." That is a lie. Words do hurt. I don't care how old or young you are. Words have a way of penetrating the soul of a person. They become the pattern for our internal voices and how we speak to ourselves. When negative voices take root, it is ten times harder for a child to adopt a positive word and extra hard work to get that child to believe they are those positive words.

The negative words I heard as a child still hurt me. At times, they replay in my mind. Trying to recover, rebuild, retrain my internal voice is challenging. Speaking with my therapist gives me a cleanse where I can just cry and release emotions, I didn't know were still present.

For so many things I set out to do, I had someone in my family that would say all the reasons why I wasn't enough or good enough. School, career choices, business ideas, marriage, children, and so many choices in between were beset with voices promoting the negative.

And it is not just placing limits on what I can do. It also takes the form of disparaging me for what I have not done or what took me longer than others to accomplish. I feel less of a woman at times because I don't have children yet. I hear, "You are 30 and not married because you have a bad attitude," "...don't cook..." "you're moody," and more. As if that is not enough, they also project, "Good thing you're not married because you would be divorced."

Addressing these negative voices and perpetrators requires clinical professional help. The challenges are so deep-seated that conversations with those you hurt cannot undo the triggers and trauma. As an adult, I have determined to live by a set of rules:

1. I release myself from ownership and responsibility for the poor patterns and behavior of others. I will not hold and take responsibility for the trauma and your abuse of me.
2. I will remove myself and set appropriate boundaries. I will not be obligated to stay in the position of your punching bag.
3. I will evaluate relationships based on treatment and purpose. Time or title doesn't determine whether and how long you should endure a relationship. If you are not being treated well, you must leave.

Making Friends

How can someone say that they have your best interest at heart, that they care and love you, but when you do something perceived as against them, all bets are off. I don't want to come across as if I'm innocent in every interaction. Yes, I've said and done some hurtful things. Yet I think some take issue with you when you stand up for yourself. I have not always handled situations with tact and precision, but people can only take so much before they SNAP.

I realized during my journey to beware of people who will seek to box you into a corner that allows them to control you. It is up to you to stretch and knock down every wall of that corner. Don't let someone tell you what you can and cannot do when it comes to your vision and dreams. No one has to understand them or be on board with you. Remember, God only needs one vessel to say yes, and he will do the rest.

You must trust the process. I know it seems long and sometimes discouraging, but the end of the road holds a harvest for you if you stay faithful. Be honest with where you are. I used to say fake it until you make it. I now recognize the value of transparency and seeking support. Be real with your process and where you are in life. Forget about what people have to say. Find helpers, mentors, and supports that will assist you right where you are.

When you understand time and seasons, you will envy no one. I have to remind myself of this daily because it is hard to see everyone be blessed as you work. Remember, you don't know their story and the road they had to cross to get where they are.

I make friends based on conversations often started by the other person. I am not the type of person that will walk up to you and introduce myself. This is my protection from being rejected. As I get older, I realize that few people are thorough and real with themselves and you. Some people want to be with you because of what you do for them. You may be a support, but you don't receive support in return.

Many would say that I look mean. I always ask what mean looks like. Some may say that I am not approachable. I see them as judgmental. I have resolved that every personality is not for every person. If you like me, cool. If you don't, that works as well. I know my approach has kept me out of relationships that could have been beneficial, but I believe it has also saved me some less than beneficial interactions. I overanalyze and outthink myself. I compare traits and differences looking for red flags and conflict rather than similarities.

We don't know what an individual brings into our lives. The key is to allow them to play their part. Refuse the inclination to make people something that they are not. Resist the need to control how a relationship operates or the purpose of it. Instead, pay attention and discern how open your circle should be according to your comfort.

We think that the people that mean us harm are on the outside. We don't always realize that it is the people that are closer to you that have the information that can be damaging for you. People we feel are inadequate are often those that change the world. Giving a chance to someone who fits the model and answers our questions with care can open us up to someone who can change our world.

In romantic relationships, I want to be with people who challenge my thinking and love me unconditionally. Even when I am mad that they corrected a behavior that is detrimental, I appreciate the value and the interest they take. Each person needs to practice grace on both sides of this equation.

My Interests and Support

I like travel and new things. I am down for whatever is fun. I also like taking naps. I don't know if I like what I like because of my childhood experiences. I remember being in Hollywood, CA going to bungie jump. I told my cousin on the way up that I don't know if I would pull the lever. I did it. My whole heart came out. And I would do it again. Relationships often feel that way for those who have endured trauma. Remember to listen to your heart and your senses.

I believe in laughter and fun and being with people who enjoy life and bring positive energy. My friends are often different from me. I have one friend who often travels on a whim. He doesn't plan or anything. He lives by the rule that you only live once (YOLO). We often talk about plans for a life after retirement. He laughs about waiting while I emphasize planning. I don't want to live without a plan. I am equally tired of regretting. I am tired of feeling left out.

When you get yourself together and realize your worth and potential, you begin to see people for who they are and how they feel about you. Pay attention to subliminal messages. Read between the lines of what people communicate to you. They say what they truly feel in words, actions, and "jokes." Shuffle your circle like a stadium. Move people from the front row when they belong in the back. Move people from the balcony to come down front. Don't be blinded by the titles in your life. Discern based on who people show themselves to be. When they show you who they are, believe them. Move in accordance to how the person presents themselves. Recurring mistakes are choices, not mistakes.

People that you need will come as you continue forward with intention. Even if they are hidden, learn to pat yourself on the back and know that you can achieve what you desire. You are doing what you do to make an impact on the world. It is not just for you. It is a universal task that must be done. If not by you, someone still must complete the task.

Chapter 11: Moving Forward

Zechariah 4:10. Do not despise the day of small things.

Looking back over my life, sometimes I wish I could go back and change so much. But as I grew and matured, I realize that changes to my journey would change my choices and my impact potential. Small beginnings mean that the heights I reach will be more impressive and inspire all the more. I still feel that I want to change sometimes, but I have to question whether I would have the same vision, capacity, or inspiration if I did not go through what I went through. I don't know that I would be as relatable to the populations I wish to serve.

My story isn't to make individuals look at me differently or even for them to feel compassion for my past. My story is for young women who have been victims of child abuse, whether sexual, mental, or physical. I want them to see that healing is more than possible. Healing is your right and an inevitability. I want them to take hold of the challenge to determine their niche, their gift, and their purpose in the world. If this is you, I suggest three things as you have experienced them in this book: God, Counseling, and Perspective. God assures that you will overcome anything you have faced. Counseling provides you with the tools to educate your deficits and address your triggers. Perspective provides a choice in every situation to see the positive and move progressively toward your goals unbothered by the speed.

God's Plan

You may not understand why God picked this journey for you or why your path had to be so different from others. But I promise, you will evolve greater and filled with purpose when you get to the other side of the desk. I am still discovering what it has all meant and how it may be used for me. What we go through is not just for ourselves. It is also for someone else.

Growing up, my heart's desire was to impact females who grew up in similar situations. I envisioned my nonprofit. I would speak to myself with this vision. Though it was far from my mind during my experience of abuse, my purpose is clearer as I age and heal. I see the pain and behaviors that I had growing up. I see their feelings of loneliness, being misunderstood, and seeking something better.

In my employment experiences, I hear stories that connect directly to the trauma I have experienced. Processing these experiences through my lens, I have created keys to creating a therapeutic space. First, allow the client to feel. Seek their expression and reflection on their experience. Allow them to feel whatever they feel.

Some say, "You shouldn't feel that way." Who says? If you dislike a person because of what they did to you, dislike them. That feeling is warranted because it is your feeling. Acting on how you feel can be problematic but being true to your feelings and recognizing your emotions is critical to exploring other options. Emotions without reflection are motivations for actions that can't be taken back. Exploring the emotions is the process of calm, intentional choice behavior that results in what you intend.

Trauma Counseling

I graduated from college and began pursuing a Master's degree in Trauma Counseling. I switched to Child Advocacy and Policy. My experience and my education suggest that another vital component of therapeutic space is the provision of information and a practical understanding of children's rights. We tend to focus on the proper behaviors and the why of choices. But the theory reveals that an awareness of rights and options has a greater impact on choice behavior. Rights and options are at least as important as interpretations and corrections of trauma response behaviors.

For example, children in the foster care system can go to college for free. The child welfare system has multiple benefits for each child involved. Yet human trafficking, gangs, and homelessness are much too typical outcomes for these children. Again, the approach is to educate each child on the options, but trauma-informed care must focus on empowerment—enhancing the ability of the child to access and initiate based on available information—than education alone. Advocacy is needed to make these changes practical, especially in black and brown communities.

Don't allow your current situation or your history of trauma to dictate your future. The challenge is to see your worth and autonomy. As you grow through healing, you will feel lonely. You will feel like you want what you want: success, achievement, or even safety right now. You will feel unworthy, incapable, out of time. You will give up and backslide. You will be discouraged. But pace, direction, and patience will get you where you want to go. Pace reminds you to keep moving no matter how slow. Direction keeps you focused on sustainable choices and refusing to sabotage your progress. Patience reminds you to keep your sights on your vision as inspiration to put in the work.

I overthink. I reevaluate. I think that God may have something different for me. But if winning was easy, everyone would win. If you did not have doubts, anxiety, and questions, you would not be human.

You may lament the fact that you still care, but caring is exactly why you are going to reach everything you desire.

Being Planted

Psalm 1:3 King James Version (KJV)
And he shall be like a tree planted by the rivers of water, that bringeth forth his fruit in his season; his leaf also shall not wither, and whatsoever he doeth shall prosper.

All trees are planted, but they don't all flourish. Psalm 1:3 means that God wants us to bear fruit in every season, no matter what happens. If you understand fruit and trees; trees can't bear fruit in each season. A healthy tree will bear good fruit.

It is true personal fortitude that will encourage you to push forward. Stay true to what you want. Plant yourself so firmly that nothing can remove you. Your roots must be so strong and stubborn that you will stand until you make it. Despite my past, I am a social worker with the state. I'm purchasing my first home.

Remember, if you can maintain your vision, you can move toward it. You are not your yesterday. You are your present moving toward a certain future. Your story will inspire other young women waiting to cross their own river of discontent. Through your perseverance and sharing, pay forward and pass down the tools you used to make it to the other side.

I will always strive to plant a seed that encourages and builds a child. They may not recognize it today or tomorrow, but the pay forward is to plant the seeds based on the good fruit we bear. Our ultimate purpose is to speak life into others through the transparency of our experience. We have not always been whole, but our lack of wholeness may give more strength than our wholeness. When we see other plants that don't have strong roots, our story of deepening our roots and resolving our trauma can encourage and sustain their deepening and their persistence.

I want each young woman to be planted—healthy inside and out. No more shallowness. No more faking the funk. Walk into your destiny and hold the crown up. Your best is yet to come.

www.ingramcontent.com/pod-product-compliance
Lightning Source LLC
Chambersburg PA
CBHW070024110426
42741CB00034B/2489